Lila and Andy learn about

Environmental Science

Protecting Earth Through Science

Kenneth Adams

Book Cover by Kenneth Adams
Illustrations and Images by Kenneth Adams
Illustrations and Images created with AI Assistance
First Edition 2025

ISBN: 978-1-998552-25-2

Inventors and explorers were all kids once, just like you!

This book belongs to:

_____

Hi there! I'm Andy, and this is my sister Lila. A while ago, we started documenting seasonal changes in our local park and uploading our photos to a citizen science app that helps researchers track wildlife patterns. Our favorite discovery so far has been photographing the same large pine tree through all four seasons and watching how different animals use it for shelter and food.

Since we're both interested in the environment, we recently visited Banff National Park in Canada. Banff is very famous for its towering Rocky Mountains, glacial lakes, and amazing wildlife. During our visit, we noticed how grizzly bears, moose, mountain goats, and even the tiniest alpine wildflowers all live in a system that depends on balance.

Every part of the park plays a role in keeping the entire ecosystem working. For example, avalanches create clearings where new plants can grow. This changes where animals can find food, which in turn affects how plant seeds are spread around. Ultimately, this impacts the entire forest.

We also learned that the bright turquoise color of the lakes comes from tiny rock particles created by glaciers grinding against mountain stone. These same glaciers feed the rivers and provide fresh water for wildlife throughout the park, from valley floors to mountain peaks.

This shows us that everything in nature works together. The study of how all living things interact with one another and their environment is called <u>environmental science</u>. Environmental scientists investigate everything from microscopic bacteria to entire ecosystems. They gather data to help them understand how what people do affects the natural world around us.

Today, we're excited to share what we've learned about environmental science and what scientists do to keep our planet healthy!

Nature's Detectives

Environmental scientists study how plants and animals live in nature. They also study how the actions of people may affect plants and animals in their natural homes. These scientists try to figure out if forests, rivers, wetlands, and other natural places are healthy or if something is wrong that may affect their ability to support life.

When a forest starts losing trees or a river's fish begin to disappear, it is the job of environmental scientists to figure out what's really happening and to try to fix the problem.

They look at soil samples to check for harmful chemicals in the ground, they test water for pollution, and sometimes they count all the different kinds of plants and animals in a specific area, to see if their numbers go up or down.

This detective work helps them identify problems before they become too large to fix.

Environmental science includes many different kinds of sciences.

- <u>Biology</u> helps scientists understand how plants and animals live and work together.

- <u>Chemistry</u> helps them find out what types of chemicals are found in air, water, and soil.

- <u>Physics</u> helps them understand how animals move around, how water flows through rivers, and why oil floats on water during oil spills.

- And <u>Math</u> helps them understand all the data they collect to figure out if problems are developing.

These scientists also work in all kinds of places around the world. Each area is different and may need special ways to study it.

Wetland researchers focus on how water levels and plant growth change over time.

Scientists studying forests look at how fast trees grow and what types of wildlife can be found there.

Marine biologists study animals and plants in the ocean.

Urban environmental scientists investigate how towns and cities affect air quality and the local wildlife.

All these different types of environmental scientists work together to identify and understand problems in nature around the world.

Everything in Nature Connects Together

One of the most fascinating aspects of environmental science is discovering how everything in nature connects to everything else. These connections work like a giant web, where changing one thing can affect many other things.

One example of these interconnected systems is food webs. Food webs describe how energy moves through the natural world by showing how plants and animals in a specific area are connected through their food.

It typically works like this. Plants use sunlight to make their own food through a process called photosynthesis. Small animals eat plants, bigger animals eat smaller animals, and when anything dies, small organisms like bacteria and fungi break it down to feed the soil. This creates a never-ending cycle where nothing gets wasted.

As an example, let's consider some plants and animals found in the forest to illustrate a typical food web. The arrows indicate how the forest plants and animals are connected by what they eat.

1. Seeds and Nuts
2. Shrubs, Berries and Trees
3. The Hoary Marmot
4. Ptarmigan
5. Moose
6. Mountain Lion
7. Beaver
8. Gray Wolf
9. Golden Eagle
10. Grizzly Bear

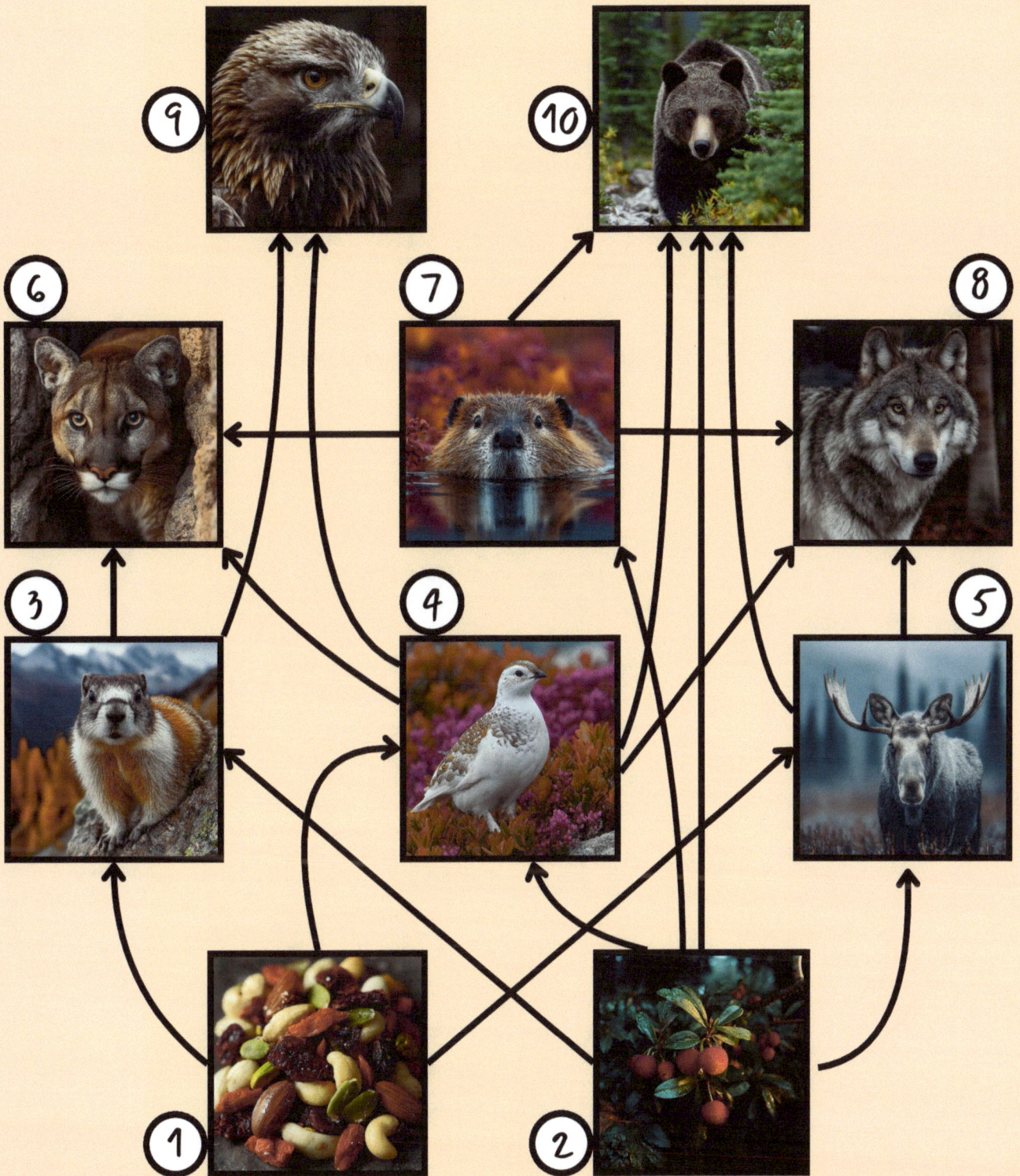

The water cycle is another example of how everything in nature is interconnected. Water evaporates from oceans, lakes, and rivers to form clouds. The water then falls to Earth in the form of rain, where it flows into rivers and lakes, and eventually back to the ocean.

While water travels through the water cycle, it gives animals drinking water, helps plants grow, and even carves out valleys and canyons in the surrounding landscape.

The Water Cycle

Water vapor condenses and forms clouds. (Condensation)

Water falls back to Earth in the form of rain. (Precipitation)

Water vapor evaporates into the atmosphere because of heat from the Sun.

Water collects in rivers, lakes, and oceans.

Environmental science matters because all these natural connections need to work well together for everything to stay healthy. When one part goes wrong, it can cause problems everywhere else. For example, if too many fish disappear from a lake, the plants they eat might grow too much. These plants can use up all the oxygen, making it hard for other animals to survive in the water.

What people do can also easily disrupt these natural connections. When people cut down big forests for wood or paper, it changes how rain forms because trees help make rain clouds. When factories dump chemicals into rivers, it can kill the fish and other animals that use the river for their drinking water. Even when we build roads, it can change how animals move around to find food and places to live.

This is why environmental science is so important. By studying how everything connects together, we can learn to understand what happens when things change. Environmental scientists use tools like computer models to help predict how humans affect nature, and then use this information to recommend ways to protect it.

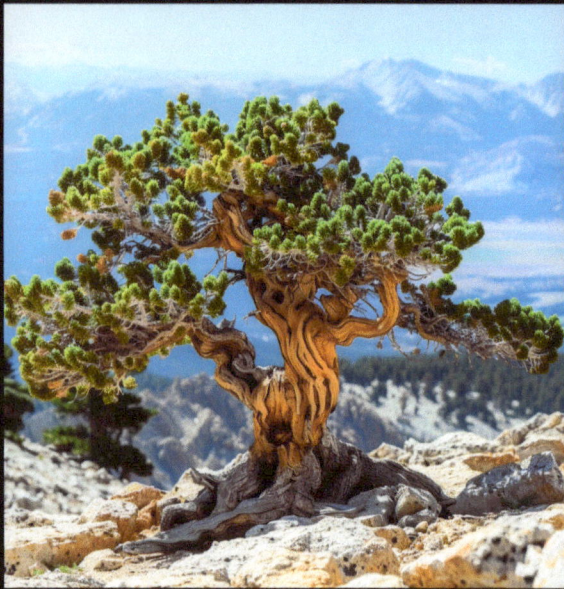

Did you know that some trees can live for over 4,000 years? The oldest known tree is a bristlecone pine in California that's been alive since before the pyramids were built!

Did you know that one drop of oil can contaminate up to 25 liters of water, which is why oil spill cleanup is so important?

Did you know that the Amazon rainforest produces about 20% of the world's oxygen and is sometimes called "the lungs of the Earth"?

Did you know that scientists have trained honeybees to detect explosives and pollution because their sense of smell is so powerful?

Signs of a Healthy Environment

Every environment has certain signs that tell scientists that everything is working well, or that there may be a problem that needs fixing. Learning to read these signs is like learning to read a secret language that nature uses to communicate.

One of the most important signs is biodiversity. Biodiversity means having lots of different types of plants and animals living together. A healthy forest might have hundreds of different kinds of trees, flowers, birds, insects, and animals.

Each living creature has a special job in the community, like pieces in a perfectly working machine. When scientists find many different species existing together, they know the environment is likely healthy.

Water quality is another thing scientists look at to see if a certain environment is healthy. Clean water should be clear and have the right amount of oxygen for fish to breathe.

Scientists test the water by looking for small organisms called indicator species. Some small creatures can only live in very clean water. Finding them means the water is healthy. Other creatures can live in polluted water. Finding too many of them might mean there's a problem with the water.

Scientists also use data collected over a long time to compare water pollution levels in different places or seasons.

<u>Soil</u> tells an amazing story about a healthy environment, too. Healthy soil is full of small organisms like bacteria, fungi, and worms that break down dead plants and animals. This creates nutrients that help new plants grow strong. Scientists can tell how healthy soil is by counting these small organisms and measuring how many nutrients are available for plants to grow.

Air quality is another important sign scientists monitor. Clean air has the right balance of gases that plants and animals need to survive. Scientists use special machines to measure pollution levels and check for harmful chemicals in the air. They also watch how well plants are growing, because plants that struggle to grow might be telling us the air isn't clean enough.

Temperature patterns also provide scientists with important information. Every living organism has a specific temperature range where it thrives best. When temperatures change too quickly or get too extreme, it can cause plants and animals to migrate elsewhere, or even kill them. Rising global temperatures caused by climate change are affecting these patterns in many ecosystems around the world.

Tools to Study Nature

Environmental scientists use amazing tools to study our planet. These instruments help them see, measure, and understand things people normally can't detect.

Water testing kits work like chemistry sets, detecting tiny amounts of different chemicals. Scientists take water samples from nature and test them by dipping test strips into the water or by adding chemical drops that change color when they find pollutants. They also use electronic meters to measure things like the amount of oxygen in the water. By looking at water under a microscope, they can count tiny living things like bacteria and algae. All these tests show if the water is clean enough for fish and safe for people.

Air monitoring stations look like small weather stations and are used to check the air quality all day long, looking for dust, smoke, and harmful gases. Some can find pollen in the air, which helps people with allergies know when the air might bother them.

Soil augers are tools used to drill into the ground and extract soil samples from deep underground without having to dig massive holes. From these soil samples, scientists can find evidence of pollution, determine the amount of nutrients that help plants grow, and find clues about what the climate was like in the past.

Scientists take pictures from high above, using **satellites and airplanes** like birds in the sky. By studying these pictures, people can learn to understand problems that are too large or occur too slowly for those on the ground to notice. For example, they can see whether forests are expanding or shrinking. They can also track pollution patterns spreading through the air and water, ocean currents moving through the seas, and ice melting at the North and South Poles.

GPS tracking devices help scientists follow animals to see how they behave in nature. Scientists put tiny radio collars on animals to learn where they go for food, water, and shelter. This information helps protect the places animals rely on for survival. Sometimes scientists even use this data to create maps showing animal migration routes.

Underwater cameras and sensors let scientists explore rivers, lakes, and oceans without getting wet. These tools can stay underwater for months, taking pictures and measuring things like temperature, how clear the water is, and what chemicals are present. This helps scientists understand what's happening underwater, where people can't easily go.

Did you know that wolves can change the course of rivers? When wolves were reintroduced to Yellowstone Park, they controlled deer populations, which allowed trees to grow back and changed how rivers flowed!

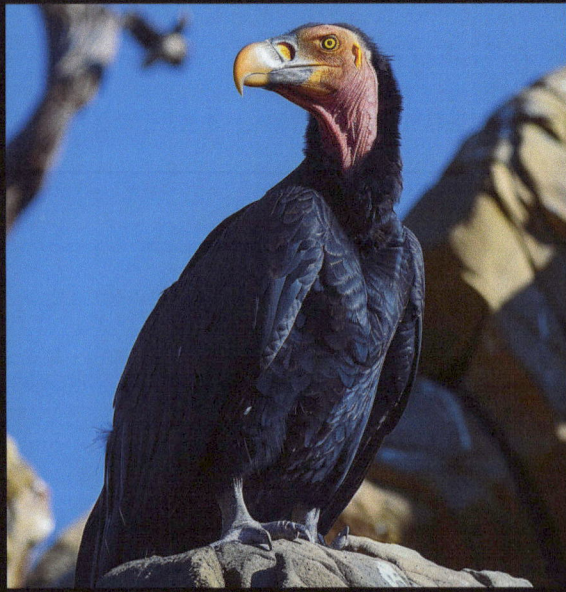

Did you know that environmental scientists have successfully brought several species back from near extinction, including bald eagles, gray wolves, and California condors, through conservation efforts?

Did you know that one large volcanic eruption can temporarily cool the entire planet by blocking sunlight with ash and particles?

Did you know that some cities are building "green roofs" covered with plants to help clean the air, reduce flooding, and provide homes for birds and insects?

Environmental Scientists at Work

Environmental scientists work on many different types of projects that help protect people and nature. These projects take them to amazing places and let them solve important problems that affect everyone. Let's explore some of these exciting projects.

Cleaning up contaminated sites is one of the most important jobs environmental scientists do. They test soil and water around old factories, gas stations, and landfills to find harmful chemicals, then design ways to clean them up so the land can be used safely again.

Asbestos removal projects help make old buildings safe. Environmental scientists test buildings for asbestos, a dangerous material used in construction long ago, and oversee its safe removal to protect people's health.

Oil spill cleanup requires scientists to act quickly when accidents happen. They study how oil spreads in water, test different cleanup methods, and monitor how wildlife recovers after the spill is cleaned up.

<u>Water quality monitoring</u> involves testing rivers, lakes, and drinking water sources regularly to make sure they stay clean and safe. Scientists check for bacteria, chemicals, and pollution that could make people or animals sick.

<u>Air pollution research</u> includes measuring smog in cities, testing air around factories, and studying how pollution affects people's breathing and health.

<u>Climate change research</u> includes studying how temperatures and weather patterns are changing, measuring greenhouse gases in the atmosphere, and predicting how these changes will affect different environments.

<u>Agricultural pollution studies</u> help farmers find ways to grow food without harming nearby rivers and lakes with fertilizers and pesticides.

Mining site rehabilitation involves cleaning up areas where companies dug for coal, metals, or other materials. Scientists test soil and water for contamination and help restore the land so plants and animals can live there again.

Wetland restoration projects help bring back marshes and swamps that were damaged or destroyed. Scientists plant native plants, restore water flow, and monitor how wildlife returns to these important habitats.

Endangered species protection involves tracking rare animals and plants, studying what they need to survive, and creating safe places for them to live and reproduce.

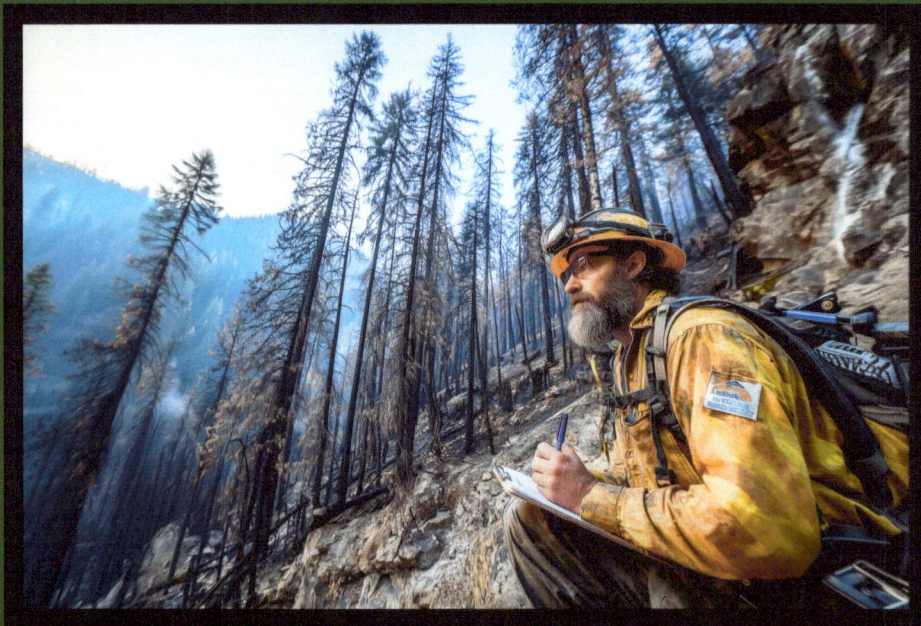

Forest fire recovery research studies how forests grow back after fires and helps land managers decide when and where to let natural fires burn.

Radiation monitoring involves testing areas around nuclear power plants and medical facilities to make sure radiation levels stay safe for people and wildlife.

Environmental impact studies happen before new roads, buildings, or dams get built. Scientists study what plants and animals live in the area and predict how construction might affect them, helping builders find ways to cause less harm.

Urban environmental planning helps cities become cleaner and healthier places to live by reducing pollution, creating green spaces, and managing waste better.

These diverse projects show how environmental scientists work to solve real problems that affect communities around the world, making the planet safer and healthier for everyone.

Environmental science shows us how amazing and complicated our planet really is.

All the different plants and animals that show if a place is healthy, the tools scientists use to check on nature, the way nature recycles water and nutrients to keep everything alive, and the scientists who work to protect our world all connect together to help our planet stay healthy.

You can also help environmental scientists by paying attention to what's happening in your own neighborhood, by noticing when certain birds arrive each spring, by watching how plants grow in different weather, or by checking if the water in a local creek looks clean or dirty. Scientists use this kind of information from people all over the world to understand what's happening to the environment.

Environmental science teaches us that people are connected to nature. When we understand our role in these systems and how important it is to keep nature healthy, we can make better choices about how we live and take good care of our planet!

Environmental Science Glossary

A glossary is like a mini-dictionary of terms with definitions.

Here's a glossary of terms associated with Environmental Science.

Air Quality - How clean or polluted the air is. Good air quality means the air is safe for people, animals, and plants to breathe.

Asbestos - A dangerous material used in old buildings long ago. Environmental scientists test for it and remove it safely to protect people's health.

Biodiversity - Having lots of different types of plants and animals living together in the same place. More biodiversity usually means a healthier environment.

Chemistry - The science that studies what things are made of and how different materials react with each other.

Citizen Science - When regular people help scientists by collecting information, like taking photos of wildlife or recording weather data.

Climate Change - Long-term changes in Earth's weather patterns and temperatures, often caused by human activities.

Condensation - When water vapor in the air cools down and turns back into liquid water, like when clouds form.

Conservation - Protecting and taking care of natural places and the animals and plants that live there.

Contaminated Sites - Places where harmful chemicals have made the soil or water unsafe. Environmental scientists work to clean these places up.

Ecosystem - All the living things (plants, animals, bacteria) and non-living things (water, soil, air) in an area and how they work together.

Environmental Impact Study - Research done before building something new to find out how it might affect local plants, animals, and the environment.

Environmental Science - The study of how living things interact with each other and their environment, and how human activities affect the natural world.

Evaporation - When water turns from liquid into water vapor and rises into the air, usually because of heat from the sun.

Food Web - A diagram that shows how energy moves through nature by showing what different plants and animals eat.

GPS Tracking - Using satellites to follow and locate animals so scientists can learn where they go for food, water, and shelter.

Greenhouse Gases - Gases in the atmosphere that trap heat from the sun, like carbon dioxide. Too much of these gases can cause climate change.

Indicator Species - Small living things that tell scientists whether water or soil is clean or polluted. Some can only live in very clean conditions.

Marine Biology - The study of plants and animals that live in oceans, seas, and other saltwater environments.

Nutrients - Natural chemicals in soil and water that plants and animals need to grow and stay healthy.

Oil Spill - When oil accidentally gets into water, harming the environment and wildlife living there.

Organisms - Living things, including plants, animals, bacteria, and fungi.

Photosynthesis - The process plants use to make their own food by combining sunlight, water, and carbon dioxide from the air.

Physics - The science that studies how things move and how energy works in nature.

Pollution - Harmful substances that make air, water, or soil dirty and unsafe for living things.

Precipitation - Water that falls from clouds to Earth as rain, snow, sleet, or hail.

Radiation Monitoring - Testing areas around nuclear power plants and medical facilities to make sure radiation levels stay safe.

Rehabilitation - Fixing and restoring damaged land so plants and animals can live there again.

Restoration - Bringing back natural areas like wetlands or forests that were damaged or destroyed.

Satellites - Machines that orbit Earth in space and take pictures or collect information about our planet.

Soil Augers - Special drilling tools that take samples of soil from deep underground without digging big holes.

<u>Temperature Range</u> - The warmest and coldest temperatures where a plant or animal can survive and thrive.

<u>Urban Environmental Planning</u> - Designing cities to be cleaner and healthier by reducing pollution, creating green spaces, and managing waste better.

<u>Water Cycle</u> - The continuous movement of water as it evaporates from oceans and lakes, forms clouds, falls as rain, and flows back to the ocean.

<u>Water Quality</u> - How clean and safe water is for drinking and for fish and other water animals to live in.

<u>Wetlands</u> - Areas where land is covered with water, like marshes and swamps, that provide important homes for many plants and animals.

Environmental Science Quiz

Multiple Choice Questions (Choose the best answer)

1. What is environmental science?
   a) The study of only plants and animals
   b) The study of how living things interact with each other and their environment
   c) The study of rocks and minerals
   d) The study of weather patterns only

2. What does biodiversity mean?
   a) Having only one type of plant in an area
   b) Having lots of different types of plants and animals living together
   c) Having no animals in a forest
   d) Having only trees and no other plants

3. How do plants make their own food?
   a) By eating other plants
   b) By drinking water only
   c) Through photosynthesis using sunlight
   d) By absorbing nutrients from animals

4. What happens first in the water cycle?
   a) Water falls as rain
   b) Water forms clouds
   c) Water evaporates from oceans, lakes, and rivers
   d) Water flows into rivers

5. What are indicator species?
   a) Animals that are very large
   b) Small creatures that tell scientists if water is clean or polluted
   c) Plants that grow very tall
   d) Birds that migrate every year

6. What do soil augers do?
   a) Plant new trees
   b) Drill into the ground to extract soil samples from deep underground
   c) Clean polluted water
   d) Measure air temperature

7. How do GPS tracking devices help environmental scientists?
   a) They help scientists find their way home
   b) They help scientists follow animals to see where they go for food and shelter
   c) They predict the weather
   d) They clean the air

8. Why do environmental scientists work on asbestos removal projects?
   a) To make old buildings safe by removing dangerous materials
   b) To paint buildings
   c) To add insulation to buildings
   d) To make buildings taller

9. What makes the lakes in Banff National Park bright turquoise?
   a) Pollution from factories
   b) Tiny rock particles created by glaciers grinding against mountain stone
   c) Blue paint in the water
   d) Special fish that live there

10. How does physics help environmental scientists?
   a) It helps them understand how animals move around and how water flows through rivers
   b) It helps them count animals
   c) It helps them plant trees
   d) It helps them cook food

11. In a food web, what happens to dead plants and animals?
   a) They disappear completely
   b) Small organisms like bacteria and fungi break them down to feed the soil
   c) They turn into rocks
   d) They float away

12. What do air monitoring stations detect?
   a) Only temperature
   b) Dust, smoke, harmful gases, and sometimes pollen
   c) Only wind speed
   d) The number of birds flying by

13. What is the main goal of cleaning up contaminated sites?
   a) To build new factories
   b) To test soil and water around old factories and design ways to clean them up
   c) To plant flowers
   d) To make the land look prettier

14. What happens when temperatures change too quickly?
   a) Nothing happens to plants and animals
   b) Plants grow faster
   c) It can cause plants and animals to migrate elsewhere or even kill them
   d) Animals become stronger

15. What is the purpose of wetland restoration projects?
   a) To build shopping malls
   b) To help bring back marshes and swamps that were damaged or destroyed
   c) To create swimming pools
   d) To remove all water from an area

16. Why must scientists act quickly during oil spill cleanup?
   a) Because oil spills are not dangerous
   b) Because oil spreads rapidly in water and can harm wildlife
   c) Because they want to go home early
   d) Because oil is expensive

17. What do citizen science apps help with?
   a) Playing games
   b) Helping researchers track wildlife patterns by letting people upload photos
   c) Ordering food
   d) Watching movies

18. What do avalanches do in forest ecosystems?
   a) They destroy everything permanently
   b) They create clearings where new plants can grow
   c) They make the soil poisonous
   d) They stop all animal movement

19. What does mining site rehabilitation involve?
   a) Digging more holes
   b) Cleaning up areas where companies dug for materials and helping restore the land
   c) Building new mines
   d) Selling the materials

20. How does urban environmental planning help cities?
   a) By making cities louder
   b) By reducing pollution, creating green spaces, and managing waste better
   c) By building more factories
   d) By removing all trees

21. Environmental science is the study of how all living things _____ with one another and their environment.

22. Plants use sunlight to make their own food through a process called _____.

23. In the water cycle, water _____ from oceans, lakes, and rivers to form clouds.

24. _____ means having lots of different types of plants and animals living together.

25. Some small creatures called _____ species can only live in very clean water.

26. When anything dies in a food web, small organisms like bacteria and fungi break it down to feed the _____.

27. Healthy soil is full of small organisms like bacteria, fungi, and _____ that break down dead plants and animals.

28. Clean air has the right balance of _____ that plants and animals need to survive.

29. _____ tracking devices help scientists follow animals to learn where they go for food, water, and shelter.

30. Water testing kits work like chemistry sets, detecting tiny amounts of different _____.

31. Scientists take pictures from high above using _____ and airplanes to study large areas.

32. Environmental scientists test soil and water around old factories to find harmful chemicals at _____ sites.

33. Every living organism has a specific _____ range where it thrives best.

34. _____ restoration projects help bring back marshes and swamps that were damaged.

35. Environmental _____ studies happen before new roads, buildings, or dams get built.

36. _____ biologists study animals and plants in the ocean.

37. Glaciers feed the rivers and provide fresh _____ for wildlife throughout the park.

38. Scientists who study forests look at how fast trees grow and what types of _____ can be found there.

39. Climate change research includes measuring _____ gases in the atmosphere.

40. _____ monitoring involves testing areas around nuclear power plants to make sure radiation levels stay safe.

41. Environmental scientists only study plants and animals, not human activities.

42. In a food web, energy flows in a never-ending cycle where nothing gets wasted.

43 Underwater cameras and sensors can stay underwater for months taking pictures.

44. All creatures can live in both clean and polluted water equally well.

45. Soil augers require scientists to dig massive holes to collect soil samples.

46. Satellites can track pollution patterns and ice melting at the North and South Poles.

47. When forests are cut down, it has no effect on how rain forms.

48. Asbestos is a safe material that was commonly used in old buildings.

49. Biodiversity means having only one or two types of species in an environment.

50. Climate change is affecting temperature patterns in ecosystems around the world.

51. Environmental impact studies happen after construction projects are completed.

52. Oil spills clean themselves up naturally without any human intervention needed.

53. Citizen science apps allow regular people to help scientists by uploading photos of wildlife.

54. Air monitoring stations only check for dust and cannot detect harmful gases.

55. Wetland restoration projects help bring back damaged marshes and swamps.

Quiz Answer Key

Multiple Choice	Fill-in-the-Blank	True/False
1. b	21. interact	41. False
2. b	22. photosynthesis	42. True
3. c	23. evaporates	43. True
4. c	24. Biodiversity	44. False
5. b	25. indicator	45. False
6. b	26. soil	46. True
7. b	27. worms	47. False
8. a	28. gases	48. False
9. b	29. GPS	49. False
10. a	30. chemicals	50. True
11. b	31. satellites	51. False
12. b	32. contaminated	52. False
13. b	33. temperature	53. True
14. c	34. Wetland	54. False
15. b	35. Impact	55. True
16. b	36. Marine	
17. b	37. water	
18. b	38. wildlife	
19. b	39. greenhouse	
20. b	40. Radiation	

Take a look at other subjects Lila and Andy are learning about...

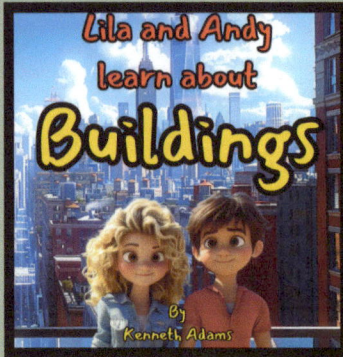

Lila and Andy learn about **Buildings**
By Kenneth Adams

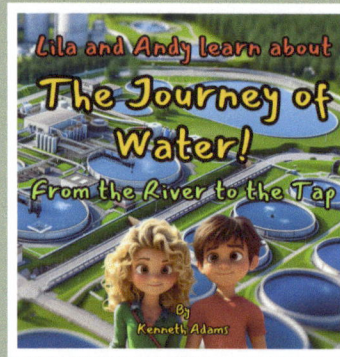

Lila and Andy learn about **The Journey of Water!** From the River to the Tap
By Kenneth Adams

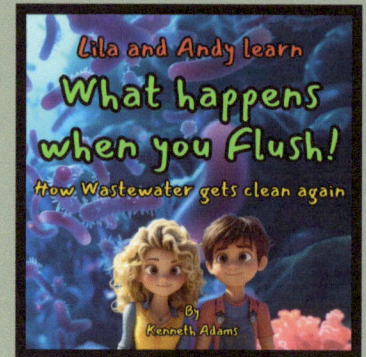

Lila and Andy learn **What happens when you Flush!** How Wastewater gets clean again
By Kenneth Adams

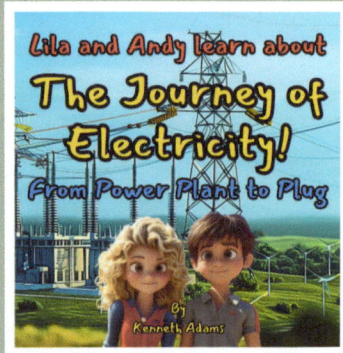

Lila and Andy learn about **The Journey of Electricity!** From Power Plant to Plug
By Kenneth Adams

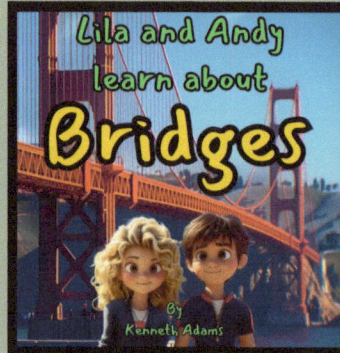

Lila and Andy learn about **Bridges**
By Kenneth Adams

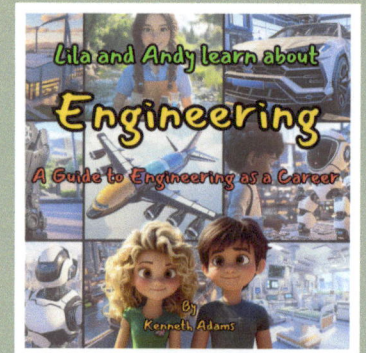

Lila and Andy learn about **Engineering** A Guide to Engineering as a Career
By Kenneth Adams

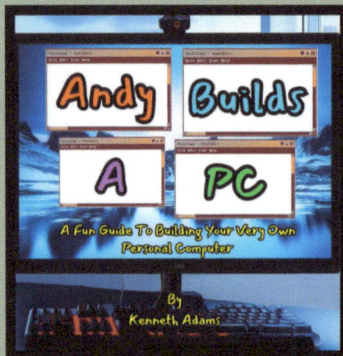

Andy Builds A PC A Fun Guide To Building Your Very Own Personal Computer
By Kenneth Adams

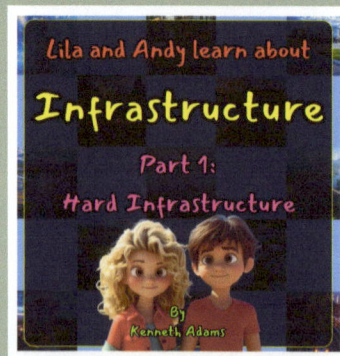

Lila and Andy learn about **Infrastructure** Part 1: Hard Infrastructure
By Kenneth Adams

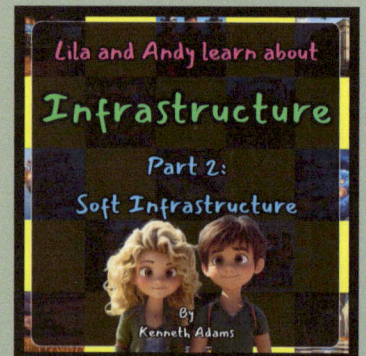

Lila and Andy learn about **Infrastructure** Part 2: Soft Infrastructure
By Kenneth Adams

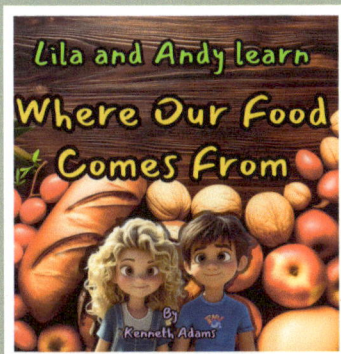

Lila and Andy learn
Where Our Food Comes From
By Kenneth Adams

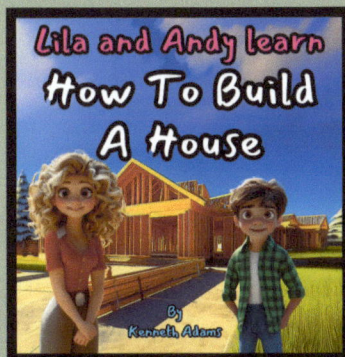

Lila and Andy learn
How To Build A House
By Kenneth Adams

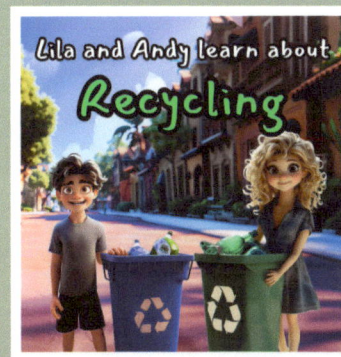

Lila and Andy learn about
Recycling

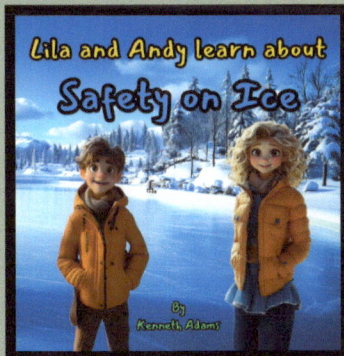

Lila and Andy learn about
Safety on Ice
By Kenneth Adams

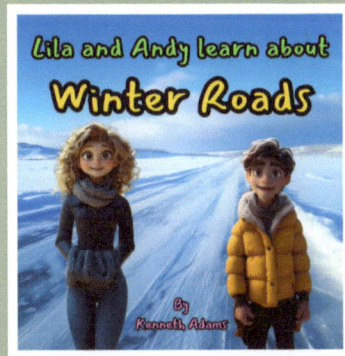

Lila and Andy learn about
Winter Roads
By Kenneth Adams

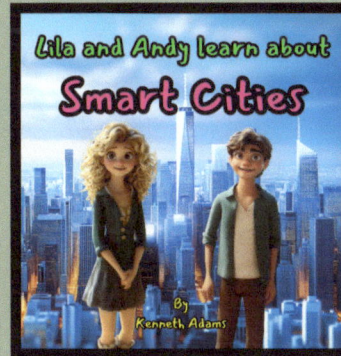

Lila and Andy learn about
Smart Cities
By Kenneth Adams

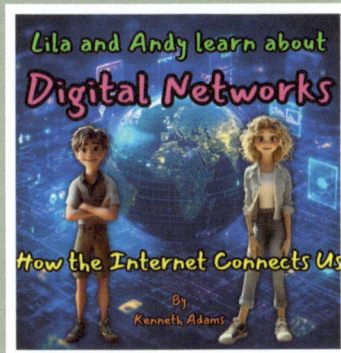

Lila and Andy learn about
Digital Networks
How the Internet Connects Us
By Kenneth Adams

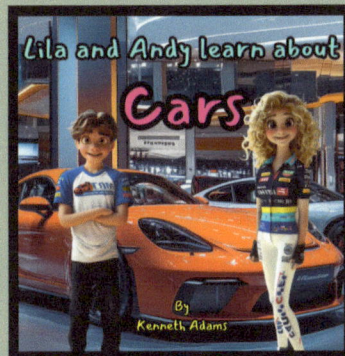

Lila and Andy learn about
Cars
By Kenneth Adams

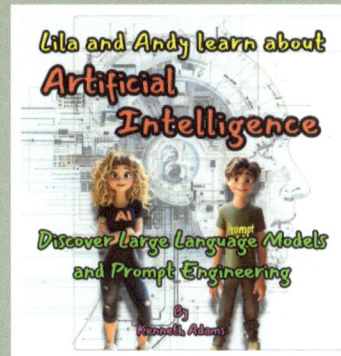

Lila and Andy learn about
Artificial Intelligence
Discover Large Language Models and Prompt Engineering
By Kenneth Adams

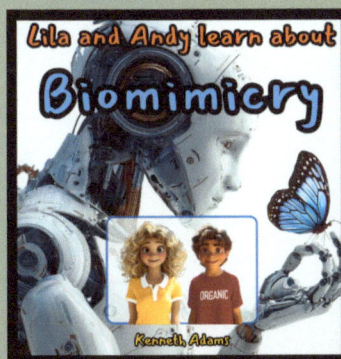

Lila and Andy learn about
Biomimicry
Kenneth Adams

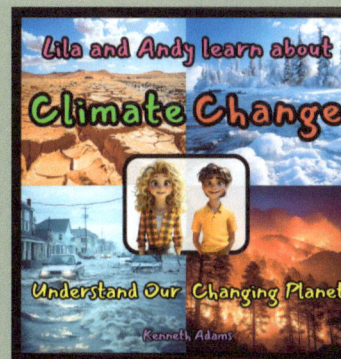

Lila and Andy learn about
Climate Change
Understand Our Changing Planet
Kenneth Adams

www.ingramcontent.com/pod-product-compliance
Lightning Source LLC
Chambersburg PA
CBHW042013080426
42734CB00003B/70

9 781998 552252